JOB INTERVIEW SKILLS

Crushing your Job Interview: the most easy steps to getting hired. A Job Seeker's Essential Guide to Interviewing Skills.

Paige Labert

TABLE OF CONTENT

Introduction

Preparing for a job interview may be one of the most significant activities you may do in your professional life. Successfully securing your dream job is not only a path toward financial stability but also toward personal satisfaction and happiness. We spend inordinate amounts of our time at work, crafting our careers, and building our skills; we should invest that time wisely in the most fulfilling job that we can possibly find.

One of the most important parts of the job search is the interview itself. This book guides you through the process of preparing for the best job interview of your career. From understanding the variety of questions, you might get to learning how to prepare smart answers, you will learn how to navigate the intricate process of successful job seeking. You will also acquire some techniques following the STAR method: responding according to situation, task, action, and result. At the end of the book, you will find a representative set of tough questions and appropriate answers to help you prepare.

After you are finished reading this guide, you should have everything you need to prepare for the interview of a lifetime. Decide today to quit languishing in an unfulfilling and unrewarding job and start building a successful career for your future happiness and well-being. Preparing for a job interview is like embarking on any other significant project: it takes knowledge, practice, and perseverance to navigate. Here you will find a full road map of how to get from where you are to where you want to be.

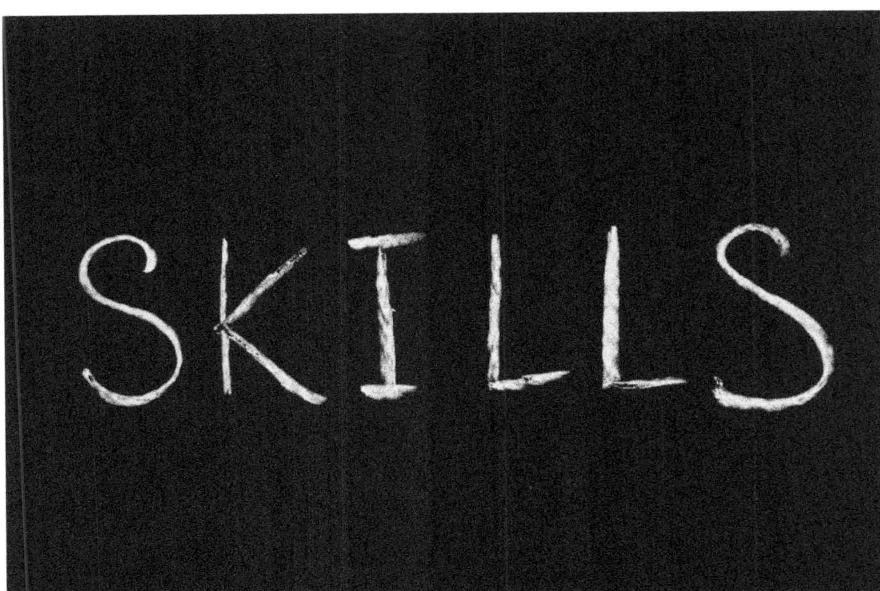
SKILLS

Chapter 1: The Importance of an Interview: Getting Your Dream Job

The process of securing and performing well in a job interview can be challenging, but it is ultimately one of the most rewarding endeavors on which you can embark: securing your ideal job is one way in which to gain entry into whatever elite group you've always wanted to be a part of. While there is no truly typical job interview—the experience encompasses too many variables (candidate, employer, field, and so on) to be wholly predictable—there are some common elements that occur in most interview situations. Understanding the basics of interviewer's categories of questions, as well as honing your ability to answer clearly and cleverly, can give you a significant advantage in the interview process. The importance of a job interview really cannot be overstated: this simple act is the culmination of your years of hard work, focus, and energy. You may have paid tens of thousands of dollars for a higher education or special training just to get to this point; you may have spent your entire life dreaming of this particular job in this particular field; you may have an inkling that this job might be able to propel you to success and security in ways you have heretofore only dreamed of.

The job interview is also a very complicated endeavor, from the pre-interview preparation to the interview itself to the post-interview follow-up. You have to remember that you are, essentially, in the process of selling yourself: you are trying to get the employer to buy your certain set of skills, both hard and soft (which will be discussed later in the book), as well as your enthusiasm and personality. The guidelines that you will review throughout the course of this book will give you the best advice on how best to sell your particular set of experiences, skills, and personality.

A job interview isn't merely a moment in time wherein you are asked some questions and demonstrate some skills: it can potentially alter the course of your life, getting the job of your dreams. Thus, it should be approached with care and thoroughness: you should prepare for a job interview the same way in which you would prepare for a great athletic event or a major performance. That is, you should not only hone your skills and learn from your experiences, but you should also practice and practice well. To show up for a job interview without fully undertaking some considered practice is to show up for the big game without any warm up at all. Your livelihood and your future depend on your career, to some extent; treat it with care and precision, as you would other facets of your life.

One of the first ways in which you can prepare adequately for an interview is to start thinking about what kinds of questions the interviewer may ask, and preparing some possible answers to potential questions. There are many standard questions that interviewers will ask, in various ways, and going over these and understanding what is being asked, as well as how best to answer is one of the most important parts of any interview preparation. The kinds of questions asked range from verification and experience questions to opinion and behavior questions, among others, and they require different kinds of in-depth preparation (see my book Job Interview Q&A for a more thorough overview of the many kinds of questions and possible answers, along with some ideas for practice). Using the STAR answering method—focusing on situation, task, action, and result—will likely net you the best responses. Much of this will be covered later in this guide.

Always be sure to bring your cover letter and resume to the interview with you, in case you need to reference something specific from your past experience or current explanations of skills. Jotting down a separate list of specific skills that you have is also a good idea to have with you, particularly if you tend to get anxious in an interview: these lifelines can help you regain your footing should you get a little nervous. Still, the best way in which to combat nerves is to prepare thoroughly, so be sure also to review both your resume and your cover letter before you come to the job. Make notes on your copies that will remind you of particular stories you might wish to tell in the context of an interviewer's question. Additionally, it is a good idea to bring a few extra clean copies of your resume and cover letter, in case there are more than one interviewer or in case the interviewer wants to pass on your information to someone higher up in the company. The same should be prepared in the case of a reference list, as well.

Also spend some time reviewing the job advertisement, so that you are as clear as you can possibly be regarding the expectations and duties of the job itself. You should be able to connect your skills and experiences directly to what is asked of in the original request for employment. Or, in the case of a career transition or promotional position, you should be able to explain how your skill set will translate to a new set of responsibilities and tasks. Find out as much as you can from as many sources are available as to what the job itself will entail; the more specifically you can address what the employer needs, the better a choice you make yourself. Show how your energy and enthusiasm to tackle new challenges will make you the best candidate.

In addition to looking at the job itself, do some research on the company itself, its culture and its accomplishments. You should have a clear idea of the company's history, its mission statement and goals, its management structure, and its products and/or services. You are not merely selling yourself as an individual, but you are also working to sell your ability to fit into a larger corporate culture and structure. This will also give you material for questions that you might have at the end of the interview; the more you know, the more prepared you are to make the best decision for yourself. To that end, you should be prepared to find out what kind of potential for growth and promotion there is available in a given position. It would be prudent to understand how this position can translate into future opportunities—this is especially important if you are starting at an entry level position. Not only does it give you valuable information for making your final decision, but it also shows your potential employer that you have ambition and goals to move from one level to the next.

Clearly, it is also prudent to ask about salary and benefits, unless this has been made specifically clear prior to the interview. In many cases, a job advertisement will post a salary range rather than a specific number, and benefits may or may not be listed. Be polite and direct when asking the question and remember to have your own threshold in mind: it is a waste of everyone's time if the salary that will be offered to you is one you will not take. Thus, approaching these things in a professional manner from the beginning is always the best method.

Finally, your attitude and professionalism are perhaps the most important things that you can offer during an interview. If your resume and cover letter have already demonstrated that you have the experience and skills to garner an interview in the first place, then what will put you over the top is your enthusiasm and knowledge of the company, the job, and your own achievements. Be prepared and eager, friendly and professional, and that ideal job is well within your reach.

Chapter 2: Interview Skill 1: Looking Professional

Certainly, any good job interview begins with an idea first impression, and that first impression is informed by how we look, in particular, how we are dressed and groomed prior to the interview. In recent years, the standards for what constitutes "business" dress have been changed and, for the most part, expanded. Still, a job interview is more than likely more formal than typical employee dress standards (especially when considering the proliferation of "casual Fridays" and tech start-ups jeans and t-shirts). Whatever the company for which you are interviewing, you should follow some basic guidelines to ensure that you are looking professional and making a smart first impression.

General Guidelines for Professional Presentation

•	In doing your company research, you should have some broader knowledge of company culture, including how employees are supposed to present themselves in the workplace. Use that knowledge to base your understanding of how to present yourself at an interview: as stated above, an interview is likely a more formal affair than an everyday work look, but it gives you a starting point. Be sure to peruse any company photos, especially on social media, to get an idea of how employees dress when they are representing the company.

•	While you are trying to look your best—professional and poised—you should also take into consideration your comfort level. That is, don't wear something that is too tight, too bulky, or too warm to an interview. The more comfortable you are in your professional attire, the more confidence you project. Be sure to take the seasons into the occasion, and wear layers if you tend to get warm during an interview; you can take off a jacket should you need to, if you are wearing a nice dress shirt or blouse underneath.

• Avoid wearing anything that is revealing, such as a sundress or low-cut blouse. This guideline doesn't at first appear to relate to men, but a vee-necked shirt or lack of socks might fall along these lines for men. The idea is not to look like you're going out with friends, but you are representing yourself professionally for a company.

• Be certain that your clothes are recently cleaned, especially if you plan to wear a suit or other truly formal attire, and check for stains, tears, or other signs of distress. If you do not have an appropriate outfit for an interview and lack the financial ability to purchase one quickly, there are many resources in communities, like Dress for Success, that will help you find something appropriate at a reasonable price—or for free.

• Lay or set out your clothes the night before the interview. This ensures that you make a good inspection of everything (if you have pets, be sure to give yourself a quick roll before you leave the house) and that you don't have any last-minute delays. One of the worst things you can do is to show up late for an interview: give yourself plenty of time to get ready and to get there on time.

• Finally, don't second guess yourself or overthink it. If you feel reasonably comfortable and have chosen a clean, pressed outfit that seems to meet the standards of the company, then you are probably going to be just fine.

Considerations for Men

• In nearly every case of interviewing for a traditional company, a suit is required, regardless of standards for an everyday dress as an employee. Again, do your research, but always err on the side of being conservative when in doubt.

• According to most experts, a dark suit with a light-colored shirt is the most standard suit attire. Be sure that you have a matching tie, coordinated socks, and a nice belt, in addition.

• Again, if you do not own a suit, now is the time to invest in one—one that fits and is comfortable, not something that you have leftover from a cousin's wedding ten years ago. If you need assistance financially with acquiring a suit, check into local organizations that help people find employment.

• Beware of loud colors or overbearing ties; certainly, you want to avoid anything that seems overly whimsical or novelty (this is not the time to wear cartoon- or NFL-patterned ties).

• Of course, you want to appear neat and clean, but also be aware to avoid strong colognes or other scents; you do not want to trigger a reaction in an interviewer. Check your nails, too, as your hands will be noticed during an interview, from your handshake to handing out of documents and such.

• Avoid smoking before the interview if at all possible. You don't want to bring in lingering smells of tobacco or other odors that might be unpleasant to an interviewer.

• Groom your hair nicely. Again, the rules for how to wear one's hair have changed dramatically over the last couple of decades, especially for men. Use your best judgment and follow what you see on the company's web site as a guide. An investment banking company will probably want to see short, conservative hair, while a tech start-up will likely not be bothered by longer or different styles.

• If you are called for a second interview, the best rule of thumb is to dress like your potential employer; this could mean being slightly less formal, but not always. At that point, you should have a good feel for the company in order to understand and integrate the culture.

Considerations for Women

• Some of the same rules apply to women: you should probably wear some kind of suit, either with a skirt or pants. When wearing a skirt to an interview, you should always wear some kind of hose rather than presenting bare legs. Typically, you should avoid open-toed shoes or sandals. Again, do your research and peruse pictures of employees on social media. When in doubt, be more conservative than not.

• Remember to make sure that you are comfortable, and practice seeing how you feel when you are sitting down; an ill-fitting jacket has a tendency to gap when you are seated, and a tight waistband on pants or a skirt will cause discomfort. Most stores offer some sort of minor tailoring to have adjustments made to what you might purchase for an interview. If your budget doesn't allow you to purchase something nice for the interview, seek out local organizations that assist people in gaining employment. There are places that will help you find something appropriate, like the Dress for Success program.

• As with the advice for men, wear something that is darker in color, avoiding bright or flashy colors and embellishments, for the most part. A dark suit with a lighter blouse is considered the standard. Never wear low-cut blouses or sheer fabrics of any kind, and make sure the length of your skirt, if wearing one, is appropriate. Conservative interviewers often complain about the length of skirts; too short is inappropriate, while too long isn't professional. Stick to roughly knee-length skirts for interview occasions.

• If you must accessorize, then be judicious: don't cover your hands in rings or wear stacks of bracelets or long, chunky necklaces and earrings. Accessories are your chance to shine, really, if you employ them properly. With a conservative suit, one nice pendant or pair of pretty earrings can really pop and make you stand out.

- The same ideas above also apply to hair and make-up: be relatively conservative. Don't wear heavy eye make-up or drastically dark lipstick; these looks aren't considered wholly professional. With hair, keep it neat and tidy—be yourself, of course—and avoid overly stylized or trendy looks (such as lavender hair or faux beehive dos). Nails should be groomed, but avoid long, overly decorated nails, especially of the trendy press-on type. Not only do these appear flashy and lack professionalism, but they get in the way of your ability to execute daily business tasks.

- When it comes to shoes, avoid the kind of shoe you'd wear out on a weekend. Keep the heel to a minimum, and be sure that the shoes are closed both at the toe and the back. A basic pump style is always available, and these comfortable yet smart shoes will virtually never go out of style. It's a good one-time investment in a neutral color, such as brown or black.

- Match your hose to your skin color, rather than wearing colorful or graphically printed tights. Remember that the goal is to draw attention to your skills, not your style.

- Obviously, you want to be neat and clean for the interview, and be sure to avoid heavy perfumes or other scents that may be overpowering for others in an interview. Don't smoke right before the interview if you can avoid it as smelling of smoke can be a negative trigger for many.

- As with the advice above for men, the guidelines for what constitutes professional dress have shifted and broadened over the last couple of decades. This is why doing your research into the company is important for you to have a clear sense of what would be the most appropriate attire. Still, it is doubtless best to err on the side of caution rather than flamboyance for an interview.

•   If called for a second interview, follow the cues that you picked up while at the first. Dress like your boss, perhaps a touch more conservatively, and you should be in line with what is expected.

Some Considerations for All

•   While your abilities and skill set are vastly more relevant to whether or not you can do the job you're trying to procure, your image says a lot about how you view yourself. It projects that you have a solid work ethic—enough that you care about how you are perceived by others in the professional space. These guidelines aren't to satisfy some bland, generic standard; they are a way for you to meet expectations while projecting a sense of responsibility and maturity.

•   Looking "good" and feeling "good" are reciprocal ideas: if you look good, then you will feel good—and vice versa. The same goes for professionalism: if you look like a professional, then you are more likely to act like a professional.

•   It also follows that feeling good is instrumental in performing well and looking professional. That is, take care of yourself by eating well, drinking lots of water, exercising, getting adequate sleep, and applying some of the stress reducers discussed in the previous chapter. Taking care of yourself is a first, big step toward looking and feeling good and professional.

•   How you are dressed telegraphs a message about who you are: think about that before your interview and beyond your professional life. What kind of message do you want to send about your persona, your capacities, and your intelligence? This should serve as a constant baseline for checking in on your workplace look.

•   Always, when in doubt (or when thrown into an unfamiliar professional situation), overdress rather than underdress. It is far better to show up to a conference in a comfortable business suit when everyone is in khakis and button-ups than it is to show up in jeans and a t-shirt when everyone is wearing a business suit. Better to be the more polished the candidate than a diamond in the (too) rough.

•   Keep your sense of personal style without overdoing it. You are an individual, after all, and the way in which you present yourself to the world is part of your identity. Just be clear that your identity should also express a sense of teamwork to your potential employer. Dressing in a standard professional way indicates you are willing to play by the rules, as it were, and be a member of a larger team.

•   Finally, remember that looking professionally is, at the base, a way of showing respect for your interviewer and for the company at which you wish to be hired. It is also a way of showing respect for yourself, presenting yourself as a confident, capable, and courteous potential employee.

Chapter 3: Interview Skill 2: Acting Professional

Not only do you need to dress for success, as it were, but you also need to put your best foot forward when attending your interview. Acting professionally consists of any number of minor behaviors and skills of etiquette. As anyone who has worked with others in any capacity before well knows, the attitude one displays and the behavior one engages in speaks volumes about personal character and professional capacity. When embarking on an interview, it is understandable to be intimated by strangers who have some sort of control over your potential future. However, now that you have snagged the interview with your sharp resume and descriptive cover letter, you need only to look—and act—the part. The following tips should help you develop your professional etiquette for the interview and beyond.

Professional Interview Etiquette

• Remember that one of the crucial tests you must pass when attending a job interview is the litmus test of whether you will fit into the culture of the company. In general terms, this means that you need to demonstrate professional etiquette and respect not only to your interviewer but toward anyone else you may encounter (other employees, like a receptionist or secretary or colleagues in your department or group). Your skills are rendered irrelevant if your behavior is boorish and rude.

- Consider your first impression; you must not only look the part but also act the part. A first impression can never be retracted, so it is important not to begin an interview on the wrong foot. From the moment you arrive at the company, be on your most professional behavior: for all you know, the person you greet in the hallway or ride in the elevator with may be your future boss or colleague. Be enthusiastic and look happy—rather than apprehensive—to be there. Make eye contact and introduce yourself politely when appropriate, extending a handshake in most cases. When entering the interview space, be sure to accept instructions politely and strike an open—rather than defensive—posture.

- As mentioned in the previous chapter, be sure that the outfit you've chosen to wear for the interview is appropriate and professional, but also be aware of how it will appear when you are seated. You want to avoid the proverbial wardrobe malfunction (gaping blouse, popped button, overly hiked pants). Typically, you will be seated for most of the interview, so that's how you should test the comforts and utility of your chosen attire.

- Always remember to smile and appear interested in what the interviewer is saying. A smile (or, conversely, a frown) can speak volumes. If you appear smiling and approachable, then you are perceived as a team player with valuable character attributes as well as professional skills to bring to the company. A frown, on the other hand, can fluster or annoy the interviewer; it is difficult to know how to interpret the facial expression. Are you angry, annoyed, bored, frustrated, or otherwise unimpressed? This is not the impression you want to convey. Remind yourself that this experience, while somewhat nerve-racking, should be an amicable way in which to showcase your considerable talents and value. This would bring a smile to anyone's face.

• Body language, in general, reveals a lot about a person's feelings and character. Crossing your arms against your chest looks defensive, even hostile, while a lazy slump indicates a lack of interest or disrespect. Keeping your hands folded in your lap throughout the interview can have the effect of implying childlike anxiety. "Man-spreading" can look aggressive or arrogant. Again, maintain eye contact when answering questions, and avoid sweeping hand gestures. You can hold a pen or pencil in your hand if it helps to center you, and this can come in handy should you wish to jot anything down. Basically, your body language should indicate that you are engaged and open, enthusiastic and polite.

• When greeting others, be sure that you have a solid handshake, somewhere between limp and crushing. A firm handshake reveals self-confidence and a courteous understanding of overall business etiquette. When meeting someone for the first time, it is considered polite to use an honorific, such as Dr. or Ms. or Mr. If the company for which you are interviewed is owned or operated by foreign nationals, then it would behoove you to do some research into the basic etiquette of the other country. Personal space is defined differently in different cultures, in addition to attitudes about how men and women behave.

• Addressing someone by their name is also a powerful piece of business etiquette that you can employ to curry respect. Everyone likes to be noticed and remembered, so try your best to remember and repeat the names of people that you meet. Should you be called in for a further interview, this considerate formality will inevitably be noticed. Still, don't sound sycophantic: continuously repeating the interviewer's name throughout the interview—"now, that's an interesting question, Dr. Jones. Let me see how I can answer that fully, Dr. Jones. Thank you, Dr. Jones"—can be annoying and patronizing.

• As you are seated for your interview—which you should be invited to do, rather than simply plopping down—place your personal items beside or underneath your chair. For everyone's sanity and to preserve your dignity, turn off your cell phone and any other device you may have carried with you. Have your resume and cover letter, along with a notepad or folder for notes, at the ready.

• If for some disastrous reason, your phone should ring during an interview, you will be called upon to do some swift damage control. Do not dare look at the phone to check (unless you truly have a life-and-death situation on your hands); simply turn it off and apologize to the interviewer. You would have to be an excellent candidate to overcome this most egregious of etiquette breaches. It's better not to take your phone in with you if you have a habit of forgetting to switch it off. And off means off, not silent.

• When leaving the interview, be sure to restate your interest in the job and your pleasure at having met everyone. Shake hands again and repeat names, when appropriate. Be sure to thank the receptionist who showed you in, if relevant. Basically, just show proper manners on your way out the door.

• After the interview, it is customary to write a "thank you" note of some sort to the interviewer or interviewers to acknowledge their time and your opportunity. More on that will be covered in Chapter 12.

Professional Etiquette beyond the Interview

The following are some professional skills that will help you to develop into the most productive and respected employee that you can be. These skills are useful in many aspects of life, from job interviews to employee and customer interactions to any other business scenario.

• Relying on a personal set of ethics and integrity will always serve you well in the workplace. Loyalty and commitment help to cement your value as a team member, as well.

• Continuous learning increases your value over time; the more skills you are able to master, the more important (and financially valuable) of an employee you become.

- Sharing your own broad knowledge with your colleagues and others in the workplace will reveal your generosity and positive attitude.

- Be sure always to be reliable and consistent: even if you don't have the most skills or the highest creative thinking, dependability and constancy are absolutely crucial aspects to becoming a long-term employee.

- Try to stay positive, even in the face of adversity. If you do make a mistake in the workplace (or elsewhere in life), take ownership of your faults and make attempts to learn from it. Nobody is perfect, of course, but the most likable and flexible of employees admit when he or she could do better, then strives to make it so.

- A skill not to be overlooked is that of proactive engagement. Instead of waiting for others to confront a gap or fix a problem, engage with issues yourself. Noticing problem areas and dealing with them saves colleagues and superiors a lot of time and potentially wasted effort. This is the kind of engagement that earns promotions and other accolades.

- Keep up with your workload with diligence and enthusiasm. Maintain your self-discipline: prioritizing and focusing on the most important work at hand is crucial to keeping a workplace organized and productive. Avoiding distractions (like random internet time) will serve you and your productivity well.

- Use whatever resources are available to you to develop your personal and professional growth. If you are diligent in your aspirations, then your success will go farther than you thought possible.

- Avoid indulging in ego, especially within team efforts in the workplace. Your role is to support the company and advance company interests. Should your own personal feelings or ethical compass become compromised by those interests, then it is time to reevaluate your position and, perhaps, look to other sources for work. Otherwise, remember that you are a member of something larger than yourself.

- With regard to the above, be generous in your acknowledgments of others' contributions. Give credit where it is due, and strive to recognize the importance of every member within a team—this is especially important if you become a part of management. Keeping morale buoyant and stable is a fundamental part of your job, and that includes maintaining the happiness and equality of those working under you.

- Understand and utilize data that is made available to you on whatever project, whether it be sales reports or customer feedback or employee evaluations. Too often, insightful data is lost amid a desire for quicker turnover or higher productivity. Without attention to the data generated by results, whole departments can lose their efficiency and valence.

- Still, even in light of the above, strive to maximize efficiency within your own work and that of your team's or group's work. If you are able to identify ways in which to save time and/or capital, then you prove yourself to be an invaluable champion of the company as a whole. This role is also one that can lead to advancement.

• Be a willing contributor to any project or effort that is within your capacity. The more you enthusiastically "pitch in" to whatever is being proposed, the more central you make yourself to various efforts to increase productivity and/or visibility.

• Be aware that your voice is important and should be heard: when there are alternatives to an initiative, let your bosses and colleagues know about them. Even if your idea isn't ultimately followed up on, you indicate your willingness to engage with complex issues and develop problem-solving skills.

• If your ideas aren't accepted wholesale, don't complain or indulge in other base emotions. Remind yourself that you are part of a team.

• The above goes for anything that happens to become an obstacle toward success, personally or communally. Start to view events and circumstances not as obstacles but as opportunities for greater future success. Keeping a positive attitude and shifting our viewpoint makes for a consistently positive workplace. Complaining or whining about issues only marks you as a negative presence and does nothing to advance the issue at hand.

• When you face challenges, you reveal the steadfastness of your character. Listen carefully to all points of view when troubleshooting and problem solving. Creating a solution takes time and effort, so demonstrate patience, as well.

• Strive to be transparent in all of your business dealings. Honesty and openness will only make you a stronger employee (and person) and will always help you to avoid problems down the line. Getting caught in obfuscation always leaves a dark mark on your performance history.

• Keep yourself and your team organized and focused. Utilize tools such as calendars and vision boards to maintain motivation and to stay on track. An organized team that has a clear goal in mind is almost always more productive.

• Finally, communication is key to all good working relationships—to all relationships, really—so be sure to keep open communication with colleagues, management, and other valuable team members at all times.

Chapter 4: Interview Skill 3: Preparing for the Interview Part I

Now that you've secured the interview and have reviewed your professional etiquette, start thinking about the specific logistics of the interview itself. There are numerous practical and psychological issues that you should anticipate before attending the interview and getting started. First, not only should you arrive on time and looking professional, but you should also anticipate practical preparations. Second, you should review your willingness to take on the job, as well as what that role entails. Third, before you show up for your interview, spend some time thinking about potential questions and practicing your proficient answers.

Practical Preparations

Besides looking at your best and arriving on time, there are a few other practical considerations for how to function at your best at a job interview. As the old canard goes, nothing beats preparation in order to elicit a good performance. The better prepared you are, the more confident you will be, and the job you desire will be well within your reach.

• Bring your resume and cover letter with you to the interview. You will want to have a copy for yourself, as well as additional copies for the interviewer or interviewers. This is just in case you need to reference something in the course of the interview, or if additional interviewers end up coming to the session unbeknownst to you. This can also assist in future interviews so that others who might end up being involved in your hiring have copies of your credentials. Of course, the company can make additional copies, but it looks professional and organized if you happen to have a few extra copies on hand. Also be sure to have a pen or pencil with you, examples of any materials that might be relevant to the position (portfolios, for example), and copies of a printed list of references with names, titles, company and contact information. Most often, you don't need to provide this information with your resume, but if you get the interview, make sure to have this ready. Also, as mentioned before, turn off your cell phone before you go into the interview. Don't just silence it, turn it completely off.

• Review your resume, cover letter, and job description before the interview. While you will have a copy of at least two of those things on hand, you should be prepared enough not to have to reference them frequently or at all. If you're not absolutely clear on your employment history and duties that you have listed on your resume, then it comes across as inept (or even potentially inflated or false). Your cover letter should have included at least one or two more personal statements about your employment history, business ethics, or mission statement: be prepared to elaborate on anything that you have discussed there. As well, review the original job description that you used to respond so that you are clearly able to anticipate how to answer questions that match your experience and skill set to what the company originally advertised.

• Clean out your purse and/or bag before you go to the interview. You don't want to waste time or to seem disorganized rooting around through your bag in order to locate any items you may need. Also, think about anything that you might need in the course of an interview for practical use—tissues, hand sanitizer, breath mints, eye drops, or other emergency toiletries—before or during the interview. It is always better to be prepared than not.

• Use the product or otherwise familiarize yourself with what the company does/makes prior to the interview. Get as much practical, hands-on experience as you can with what the company does overall, in addition to what you yourself have applied to do specifically. Understanding the product will allow you to be able to take the first steps toward learning how your role can enhance that product's viability or marketability. An interview isn't time for a critique, of course, but it is a time to show that you are aware of the product value and how your skills can contribute.

Job Requirements and Skill Review

Aside from the practical considerations of what to bring and what to ask before the interview, you will also need to prepare some information that will undoubtedly come up during the interview. Being ready with these answers helps you to feel calm, confident, and fully prepared even before any questions are asked.

• Know the job inside and out before you arrive. That is, you should understand as fully as possible what the job requirements are for the position. If you have only a short description from the original advertisement, see if you can find out more detailed information from the company web site, social media, or a contact within the company. The more you understand what the ins and outs of the job entail, the better able you are to think about how to match your skillset to those requirements. Also, think about why it is that you want the job; that is, think about why you are best for the position, of course, but it is advantageous to display some enthusiasm about why it is that you are truly excited about the prospect of working in this particular capacity for this particular company. A little bit of genuine enthusiasm goes a long way.

• Know your audience before you come to the interview, if at all possible. Find out who will be interviewing you and do some specific research on them, if available. The more you know about your interviewer(s), the better equipped you will be to anticipate what kinds of questions they will ask and what kind of expertise they are looking for. This information should give your confidence a boost, knowing (at least to a degree) what you are walking into.

• Ask about the interview, as different companies will employ different kinds of interviews: it could be a one-on-one interview with a boss or a human resources manager—knowing which it will be should help you know how to prepare. A direct supervisor will likely want to know more specific details on your specific skill set, while a human resources interviewer will likely ask more general questions about your fitness for the company culture and team structure. Other companies will employ committees or teams to interview you, which means that you should be prepared to answer a wide range of questions. Finally, it is completely fair to ask what kinds of questions might be addressed at the interview (see more on that below), so that you can be prepared with some potential answers in advance.

•   Review your skills and be sure that you know how to elaborate on their applicability to the particular position. Be sure that you can adequately explain how a particular skill—effective communication, for example, or past leadership experience—connects with a specific job requirement. As with resumes and cover letters, throwing out these timeworn phrases is ultimately meaningless if you don't have any idea how they will connect with the real-time, practical demands of the job. For example, you might suggest that your effective communication skills will serve you in leading a team via clear, concise and consistent email threads or will assist you in creating newsletters or memos for the department or will be crucial to your ability to generate efficient reports for management. Each skill that you listed on your resume should be applicable to a particular facet of the position for which you are interviewing. Those practical connections show that your skills have concrete value and make you a more memorable candidate.

Potential Questions, Proficient Answers

Other than researching the company and outlining some stories for your interview, you should also spend some time anticipating potential questions and devising proficient answers. There are several kinds of questions that interviewers might ask and being prepared, in some form or fashion, for each type of potential question will mean that you are not unpleasantly surprised or unprepared for anything. For an in-depth look at interviewing techniques, types of questions, and how to prepare proficient answers, see my book Job Interview Q&A. For a brief explanation of this part of the interview process, see below.

• Be prepared to respond to the inevitable "tell me about yourself" opener. Generally speaking, one of the first responses that interviewers might prompt is an open-ended dissertation on yourself. This question is a kind of litmus test, an ice breaker, and a jumping-off point all in one. First, it reveals whether or not you are comfortable and prepared. Second, it functions to allow everyone to settle in a bit and relax before getting into the specific nitty-gritty of the interview. Third, it is a chance for the interviewer to discover something about you that he or she might wish to follow up on. Thus, this seemingly off-hand prompt is actually an important initial component to many interviews; have an answer ready to go, focusing on the aspects of yourself that relate to the job position, as well as being genuine and interesting.

• Credential questions will ask you to elaborate on your educational experience, any certifications or other licenses you may have acquired during the course of your previous experience, or positions of leadership you may have held. You should be prepared to discuss specific aspects of your credentials, such as classes taken or conferences attended—anything relevant to how you achieved the degrees, certificates, licenses, or other accolades that you have earned. This is not about work experience, but about your diligence and perseverance in gaining the accreditation needed to fulfill the expectations of certain positions.

• Experience questions will ask you to elaborate upon your past work (or volunteer or intern) experience. These kinds of questions prompt you to think about how you interact with others, how readily you respond to expectations and/or pressure, how well you organize and communicate, or how effectively you produce and/or work with a team. This is where you want to come up with a story or two about overcoming obstacles, solving problems, increasing productivity, or otherwise initiating innovation in your past experience. It also sometimes gives you a chance to discuss a passion project that you've undertaken in the past, either via work, interning or volunteering.

- Opinion questions will ask just that: your opinion on either an abstract issue or a concrete fact/problem/event. These kinds of questions ask you to comment on issues within your industry or regarding your past work experience. They often require you to make ethical judgments and to explain how you might respond in a given situation. These questions are both an opportunity to reveal something significant about your overall character, as well as how you might respond to difficulties or pressure.

- Behavior questions will ask what you would do in particular scenarios, as well as prompting you to provide an overarching template of how you operate in a professional setting. These kinds of questions might ask how you would solve a particular problem or how you worked to reach a specific goal. Conversely, these might ask you to describe how you overcame a stressful situation at work or how you responded to a setback. This would be an opportunity for you to indicate how one or more of the items listed in your skillset would be applicable to a real-time situation in the workplace.

- Case studies questions are usually particular to one specific interview, wherein the interviewer(s) will present a scenario to the potential candidate, then allow the candidate time to study the case before performing an analysis of the situation and projecting results or offering advice on how to render the best possible outcome. This is the kind of interview you would usually be informed about in advance.

•   Brain teasers questions are quick-fire questions that test specific skills or analytical abilities. In certain cases, you might be asked to perform mathematical problems or solve logic puzzles. In other cases, you might be asked to demonstrate proficiency in a task associated with the industry. For example, before an interview as an editor, you may be asked to take a grammatical test or review a sample submission using editorial marks.

•   Also, you should prepare some questions of your own prior to the interview. You might have some questions with regard to company practices and policies, product research and development, the logistics of your department, or salary and benefits. Prepare a list of these in advance, as most interviewers will allow some time in the end for your questions. Be cautious with regard to questions of salary and benefit, especially if not dealing with a direct superior. They may only have enough information to give you ranges or broad ideas. In addition, the question might come back to you, so be prepared to present a range, from the baseline of what you will accept to the high end of what you desire. Also, think of how badly you want the job: if you will only accept the job if it comes with a certain salary and benefits, make this clear upfront.

•   Finally, a bit of practice prior to the interview. Practicing your answers aloud in front of a mirror gives you some idea of how ready you are to respond, or you can practice with mock interviews, should you have friends or family who'd be willing to help you out. If you plan to throw out specific information for any of your answers—numbers, dates, statistics, examples—be sure to memorize these. Jot down notes on an interview preparation sheet for you to review.

Chapter 5: Interview Skill 4: Preparing for the Interview Part II

Not only will you need to think about your own skills and qualifications for the position, but you will also need to be prepared for what others might expect from you. This is why the research recommended previously in this guide is so important. Additionally, in the end, you want to approach the interview with genuineness and honesty, as personality and character are crucial components of what interviewer(s) are ultimately looking for in a candidate. Finally, there are some common pitfalls that you will want to avoid when participating in the interview; a partial list of these below should help you anticipate these and sidestep them when necessary.

Understanding Expectations

Not only should you review your own skills and qualifications, but you should also consider what hiring managers often have in mind when interviewing candidates. Understanding these expectations can help you generate potential responses that hit the mark for what management is looking for.

•   First of all, consider the position itself: what managers will expect depends largely on the nature of the job and the experience and skill set needed to fulfill that job. Thus, if you are looking at an entry-level position, then the expectations for lengthy job experience or leadership roles will be lower. In this case, it is likely that you are just embarking on your career, and so other parts of your resume will be more significant, such as educational accomplishments and other extracurricular achievements. If you are looking for a job in management or a highly technical or specialized field, then you can expect that interviewers will be looking for specific details on your abilities and accomplishments within that particular field. The position for which you are interviewing plays some role itself in understanding the expectations that hiring managers will have of you.

• Following on the above, however, employers looking to hire new workers will be much more interested in how they have demonstrated effectiveness in past work experience, rather than in educational achievements—unless you are seeking a truly entry-level position. So, emphasizing your experience, especially with regard to some of the top skills that employers are looking for (see the following chapter for more on that), will be the most significant way to impress upon them that you will be a smart choice.

• Also, remember that you are likely competing with several other candidates for the job: think about what in your past work experience makes you stand out. You'll want to be sure to prepare at least a couple of answers that demonstrate your unique abilities and how they are applicable to the current position being offered. Basically, you need to sell yourself as the best applicant for the job.

• Within that set of unique skills that you are presenting, you want to emphasize what managers might call "hard" skills:

these are the particular technical skills that are required for the job, whether it be in teaching or tech development. "Soft" skills, such as effective communication and a team-building attitude, should be on display during the interview, as well, of course. But what might set you apart from the other candidates is a surplus of expertise in a particular arena (for a teacher, say, you might have published case studies in your field; for a graphic designer, say, you may have developed new software that enables easier manipulation of features).

Conducting Yourself with Authenticity and Honesty

No amount of technical expertise or an enthusiastic report will guarantee you any job if you are not conducting yourself with integrity. If you lie on your resume or exaggerate your accomplishments, then you are likely to be exposed in the course of the interview itself—or once you're on the job, which could lead to an embarrassing and impactful dismissal or demotion. It is imperative that you come across as genuine and honest in all your professional dealings.

- The conundrum of how honest to be during the application and interview process is a fraught one: some advice out there suggests that you be honest . . . but not too honest, that it's acceptable to bend the truth a bit in the service of your ideal job search. Other advice suggests that managers and employers are truly seeking the most honest and forthcoming individuals for their positions. So, which advice is best? Certainly, the old canard "honesty is the best policy" applies to just about everything you do in life; the consequences of getting caught up in falsehoods could do more damage than even the "harmless" fib you peddled in the first place might. It reveals volumes about a person's integrity when lies are exposed, even if they are minor ones—sometimes especially if they are minor ones ("why would she lie about something so minor? What's wrong with her?"). Thus, it is always best to err on the side of truthfulness than not. However, that doesn't always indicate that you have to reveal every single thing about your work history or experience: everyone makes mistakes, and if you have learned from them, it might be an advantage to bring such issues to light in an interview (indeed, many interviewers will ask outright to talk about past mistakes and how you dealt with them). But, everyone also deserves to be defined by aspects of their life besides their mistakes: a particularly damaging or difficult time need not be put on the table unless it becomes highly significant to the conversation or position. Know the difference between revealing that you were fired for a mistake that you've since rectified and keeping quiet over an incident with office politics that might be misinterpreted outside the culture of your former company.

•   Nevertheless, it is never appropriate to list a certification, license, or other accomplishments that have subsequently been revoked for some reason. Even if the accomplishment in question isn't relevant for the position to which you applied, it is still unwise to elide the full truth. It is likely that the most casual search will reveal your "lie of omission," which will almost certainly knock you out of the running for the job. Additionally, claiming licensure for certain positions that you no longer have is considered a criminal act in many cases.

• Another simple reason not to elide the truth when discussing your history, your achievements, or your personal qualities is that it can lead to dissatisfaction in the job should you get it. For example, if you claim that you enjoy working with teams and emphasize your past experience with groups, but you really would rather work on your own as an individual, then obtaining a position wherein you are required to work with others regularly would be unpleasant at best. In addition, if you are hired based on the fact that you indicated that you truly enjoyed the success that comes out of hard, meaningful work, then realize that your work-life balance is being compromised, management might see quickly that you aren't actually a good fit for the job. Emphasize the character qualities and work skills that you actually possess and are positive about—this ensures that you get the job that you want and become the employee that managers need. Sometimes you might not get an offer by presenting your work style and achievements honestly; however, it is certain that you will, ultimately, get the job that is the best fit for you.

• Some common areas in which candidates elide the truth are actually opportunities to show what an exceptional employee they can eventually be. For example, when asked about "weaknesses" in the workplace, you might get uncomfortable, not wanting to reveal your shortcomings in your desire to present yourself as the best candidate. However, revealing your vulnerabilities can often make you seem more relatable and open: clearly, nobody is perfect and pretending you don't have weaknesses looks aloof and arrogant; interviewers like to see that you are self-aware and willing to improve. For another example, when asked about how you handled a difficult situation at work offers you the opportunity to show how you actually work through adversity: instead of telling the interviewer that you handled everything with smooth aplomb, revealing what was challenging for you in the scenario and how you overcame those challenges shows that you are a problem-solver and a determined employee. For a final example, the touchy subject of why you were fired always seems like a landmine, but it can be another opportunity to reveal something positive about yourself overall: if you take the attitude that "nothing was my fault," this shows you to be potentially immune to critique and perhaps difficult to work with. If you admit and accept at least some of the responsibility for what occurred, then you reveal that you can overcome difficult situations and are resilient enough to learn from bad experiences and become a better future employee. Thus, there are numerous occasions when honesty—however painful—might indeed give you an advantage.

When Interviews Go Wrong

In any stressful situation, there are bound to be impediments toward pulling off perfection. A job interview is filled with a plethora of potential to make little mistakes that might harm your prospects overall. Many of these minor landmines can be avoided with just a little bit of insight, preparation, and self-awareness, as we have discussed in the previous chapters. However, you are not the only participant in the job search prospect, and an interview might reveal some troubling "red flags" about your potential employer, as well. Securing the ideal job is as much about finding the right position at the right organization as it is about being prepared and skilled. When you attend your interview, also be on the lookout for certain signals that indicate that this company may not be the one for you. After all, with this guide to assist you—your professional resume, concise cover letter, and interview preparation techniques—the ideal job is just around the corner—and it isn't about settling. Keep looking (assuming you have the resources to do so) should you encounter some of the following issues.

•   If your interviewer doesn't seem to be perfectly clear on what the position entails or what your responsibilities might be, then this is a clear sign that there is some miscommunication or disorganization within the company itself.

•   If your research prior to the interview reveals a rosy public image with satisfied employees and customers, but your experience at the company and during the interview seems at odds with that, then perhaps you should reconsider. The public image of a company might not always live up to its actual culture; this is a time for you to use your best judgment about what's in your best interests.

• If your interviewer doesn't seem engaged with your answers or asks only a repetitive set of generic questions, then it is likely the case that either the company has already determined who they will hire (hint: it's not you) or the position is a redundant one, mostly unimportant to the workings of the company. This might indicate that prospects for advancement are low or non-existent.

• If the research you conduct on the company indicates that leadership is in flux, is floundering, or has a high rate of turnover, then this is a clear red flag that something is wrong at the core of the company itself. You don't want to chain yourself to a sinking ship, as it were.

• The same consideration applies to your understanding of the company's mission statement. If their mission seems unclear or contradictory, then that's an indication that the company is in trouble or in a rut.

• If your interviewer seems unprepared, then you should reconsider, as well. Again, this reveals a lack of organization and clarity within the company; or, if the interviewer will be your direct supervisor, it reveals an indication of their habitual work practices—and that might be frustrating for you in the end.

• Finally, if the process of interviewing feels too drawn out—it's taken months to get from resume to interview to follow-up interview—then it's another red flag that indicates disorganization, indecision, or other core problem.

Chapter 6: Interview Skill 5: Demonstrating the Top Skills

If you are working on your resume, cover letter, and interview preparation, then you will definitely want to know what employers are looking for the most. While each individual job will have its own special set of requirements and unique attributes, there are certain kinds of skills that every employer seeks in just about every employee. This isn't to say that you have to possess each and every one of these skills—that would be nigh impossible—but it is to give you some guidelines to see what employers are typically expecting and how you can showcase your experience and skillset to best meet those expectations. Usually, skills are broken down into soft skills—the kind of skills that any employee regardless of training or experience will have to some degree—and hard skills, which are the specific technical and professional expertise necessary to perform particular kinds of jobs. Additionally, there are some extraneous skills that aren't necessarily categorized as "soft" or "hard," but they are skills that will set you above many other candidates. See below for details on the top skills for which companies and managers are searching.

Soft Skills

These skills are the character attributes and personal qualities that a candidate brings with them to the position. These personality traits and behavioral standards are what allow an employee who has standard hard skills to gain an advantage over other candidates. Managers look for soft skills because no matter how good you are at executing tasks or effectively producing if your interpersonal or communication skills are lacking, then you are likely not the best person for the job. Soft skills are also transferrable skills, appropriate in any workplace scenario, meaning that an employee with excellent soft skills is flexible and useful in almost any position. These skills are gained not through formal training, by and large, but via personal experience and self-awareness; because they are gained over time, the employee with solid soft skills adds value to a company beyond their basic functions. Soft skills demonstrate diversity and broadness of experience, as well as attention to detail and openness to others.

• Adaptability is crucial to being able to work in any environment with diverse personalities, changing responsibilities, and varying production requirements. The more an employee is able to adapt to shifting scenarios, the more valuable she provers herself.

• Attitude cannot be understated. Employees who are able to demonstrate positive attitudes and determination, even when faced with challenges, are clearly not only valuable in what they can offer in production but also in how they can create a comfortable, calm, and welcoming environment.

• Communication skills are crucial to any job that you might encounter, including oral, nonverbal, written, and aural. Your ability to communicate effectively can make you an invaluable part of any group of companies. Your communication style should be empathetic, open-minded, respectful, and precise, depending on the situation. Listening is just as important as speaking in a communication situation. Understanding your audience also determines how you approach communication; how you speak to a customer is different than how you might speak to a colleague or a boss. And, even in an increasingly technological age, written communication skills are valuable, for emails, interoffice memos, marketing purposes, reports, production schedules, and so on. Learning to write correctly and concisely makes you a better candidate.

• Conflict Resolution can be an extremely important skill to possess, particularly in companies wherein employees work closely together in teams. This skill implies a variety of attributes that allow you to resolve issues as they arise, including mediation, empathy, facilitation, creative problem-solving, and accountability. There are even entire positions within organizations that are dedicated to conflict resolution capabilities, but this is a valuable skill for any employee.

• Creative Thinking is another broad soft skill that includes a variety of attributes, such as analytical abilities and effective communication. Creative thinking also requires an open mind to see problems and opportunities from different angles, as well as organizational and leadership skills to see them through.

• Critical Thinking is distinct, though not completely different, than creative thinking. Critical thinking skills imply the ability to make unbiased observations; provide appropriate analyses and interpretations; process issues through reflection and evaluation; inference underlying subtext; offer explanations, and employ problem solving and decision-making skills. An employee should also be able to apply critical thinking skills independent of direct guidance. Critical thinking is applicable to any and all scenarios in your professional and personal life. The ability to think critically is vital to success.

• Decision Making is a key component of critical thinking overall and reveals an independent, well-informed, and decisive employee. Good decision-making skills indicate that a candidate is knowledgeable and authoritative.

• Flexibility makes an employee more valuable because he can accept more responsibilities, accomplish a wider variety of tasks, and generally contribute to a larger degree in the workplace as a whole. Flexibility requires both a diversification of skills and an attitude of openness.

• Interpersonal skills are crucial to communication, of course, and show an employee's ability and willingness to interact with others. This includes high degrees of empathy and tolerance, as well as emotional intelligence and a sense of self-awareness.

• Leadership reveals an ability not only to perform required tasks but to step up and take on roles of greater responsibility. Showing leadership requires effective communication (including, crucially, the ability to listen to feedback), a high level of motivation to take on more responsibility, and the ability to organize and delegate tasks and functions. Leaders are also generally trustworthy and creative, with strong interpersonal skills.

• Motivation is inherent to leadership, of course, as well as to success in everyday working situations. Motivation is a highly interior attribute, as external motivations such as praise or financial reward often don't last beyond the initial payoff. Motivation constitutes an internal desire to do better and be more effective. Highly successful people are nearly always highly motivated by personal goals and ideals.

• Networking is part of our interpersonal skill set, but it is distinct in a couple of ways. It requires an ability to observe and foster connections between disparate groups of people or organizations—seeing patterns and how these interact—as well as an extroverted ability to connect to strangers and promote your interests.

• Problem Solving employs a variety of soft skills. It includes the ability to analyze a situation, generate possible responses, evaluate which response will be most effective, implement a coherent plan, and assess final results.

• Teamwork is both an interpersonal skill and a hallmark of attitude. It requires effective communication skills, including respectful listening, reliability within the team itself, and conflict resolution attributes.

• Time Management is important to any professional or personal set of tasks. Deadlines and goals may not quite be the same thing, but without the boundaries of time, not much gets done. The ability to prioritize, set a schedule, keep organized, and maintain a balance between work and rest is absolutely crucial to any employee.

• Work Ethic implies that you have the ability to be self-directed and motivated to be on time, be prepared, and be willing to get the work done when and as it needs to be done.

Hard Skills

In order to be successful at any job, an employee needs to demonstrate a combination of soft skills, as detailed above, and hard skills. Hard skills are the technical and professional skills that are gained through specific education and training. This is the expertise you have gained through formal education and hands-on experience, specific to each particular field or job. This includes not only formal education and technical training, but also apprenticeships, internships, continuing education, certification or licensing programs, and on-the-job experience. Hard skills are easily evaluated through objective definition and measurement. Some hard skills that are used in particular professions are listed below.

- Accounting
- Administrative
- Analytics
- Automotive
- Banking
- Carpentry
- Computer
- Construction
- Data
- Design
- Editing
- Electrical
- Engineering
- Financial
- Hardware
- Healthcare
- Information Technology
- Languages
- Legal
- Manufacturing
- Math
- Mechanical

- Medical
- Nursing
- Optimization
- Pharmaceutical
- Pipefitter
- Plumbing
- Project Management
- Programming
- Research
- Reporting
- Science
- Software
- Spreadsheets
- Teaching
- Technology
- Testing
- Translation
- Transcription
- Word Processing
- Writing

Other Skills

Besides the categories of soft and hard skills, employers are often looking for some miscellaneous skills that can be integrated into your responsibilities to ensure that you are a more efficient and productive employee. These additional skills highlight your ability to diversity within the workplace, adding value to whatever department in which you work. Most of these skills are technologically oriented, though not all.

•   Obviously, basic computer skills are a requirement of virtually every job in today's workplace environment. In fact, listing "computer skills" on a resume is a virtually meaningless act, given that the wide range and level of expertise within the broad category of computer skills is vast and nearly indefinable. Still, indicating that you have proficiency with particular computer skills is valuable to any employer and should be mentioned at some point in the hiring process. Should you possess particular, higher-level computer skills, this may warrant mentioning on a resume. Computer skills can be broken down into some basic attendant categories:

o   Productivity software: this includes the Microsoft Office suite of programs, which any employee should be able to maneuver at least at a basic level (Word, Excel, and PowerPoint). You should also know how to utilize and manage email, as well as digital calendars (often included within email platforms). Digital message, video conferencing, and cloud management software are other forms of productivity software that you might be called upon to use. Again, there is no need to mention these skills on a resume; wait until you are asked about them.

o   Digital marketing: this runs the gamut from web site design and maintenance to social media campaigns and has become integral to most modern companies wishing to grow a customer base. These skills include web site design, social media management, CMS and CSS knowledge, familiarity with digital media marketing and search engine optimization, as well as web site analytics. If you possess any of these specific skills and they are relevant to your position, do mention them on your resume.

o   Computer programming skills are in high demand, as well. If you are well-versed in such computer languages as HTML and JavaScript, then you should most definitely mention this. Other programs include C++, Python, and knowledge of open source software such as Linux and Unix.

o   Graphic design is another computer skill that adds value to an employee in this technological age. Familiarity with the Adobe suite of products, desktop publishing, or video creation software should be mentioned on a resume, as well.

o   There is also a demand for people with IT troubleshooting skills, though this expertise would likely be required for specific jobs rather than general application. Systems administration, server maintenance, and help desk abilities, along with various other tech support capabilities, are in great demand.

o   Cybersecurity skills are a rapidly growing field, as well, though again is mostly specialized. An understanding of malware, data encryption technologies, and virus protection software is also in high demand.

• Social media skills, as distinct from general computer skills, are becoming more and more intertwined with business needs. Like computing skills, social media skills cover a broad range of particular abilities and expertise. Social media skills can also refer to more traditional means of disseminating information and conducting marketing.

o Writing concise, correct, and engaging copy is a social media skill that is useful from blogging to web site content to marketing campaigns and beyond. Technical savvy with enormous platforms like Facebook and Twitter can be advantageous to any small company or start-up.

o Content creators need not be only writers: candidates with graphic design abilities or video creation skills are also needed to maintain a viable social media presence. Both writing and visual content creation require good editing skills.

o Public speaking is a valuable skill for many employees: being able to present a report or deliver a motivational speech can be an excellent resource for your company.

o Customer service skills also require social networking and interpersonal skills that can be crucial to the success of product-oriented companies. If you have spent time honing your customer service capacities, then you should definitely make note of that.

• Language ability is another valuable skill that can showcase your flexibility as an employee. Spanish language skills are probably the most valuable in general terms, while other languages may be important in particular fields or for multinational corporations.

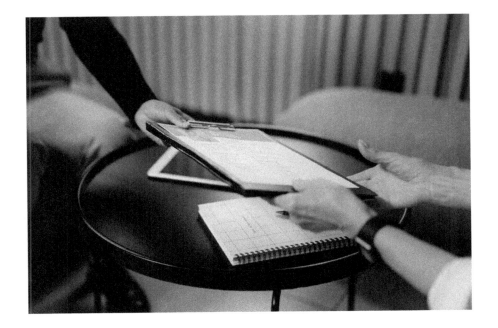

Chapter 7: Interview Skill 6: Listening and Follow Up

While most of any job interview will be primarily focused on you and what you have to say, don't make the mistake of forgetting that listening is also an important part of the process. You are also in the process of gathering information from the interviewer and from the company itself while you are vying for the position. Listening can be just as valuable as speaking, ultimately. In addition, when the actual interview is finally over, this doesn't mean that you are completely finished with the hiring process. There are important guidelines to meet when following up with the interviewer and potential employer, as you will discover here.

The Art of Listening

It is potentially the case that listening is one of the most underestimated skills that are necessary for a job interview. Showcasing solid listening skills will make you appear empathetic, engaged, intelligent, and enthusiastic. While you should certainly practice your answers to potential questions as detailed earlier in this guide, you should avoid spouting off practiced answers without truly listening to what the interviewer is requesting. An interview should have an ebb and flow like a conversation, and while much of it will be focused on you, be sure to allow yourself time and space to listen and absorb what is going on at the other side of the equation.

•   Coming with a list of prepared answers and follow up questions just isn't quite enough. As stated above, be sure you are responding to the specific questions asked during the interview, rather than trying to force your prepared answers to work on the spot. With regard to your list of prepared questions, be aware that this offers you an important opportunity to engage with your interviewer about what is in your best interest. When the interviewer(s) ask about your own set of questions, don't simply reel them off like a quick checklist. Ask a clear question and really listen to the answer, jotting down notes and reactions as you go. Oftentimes, a response to your question will lead you to a follow-up question or raise a concern or cement a positive assumption. In addition, the kinds of questions that an interviewer asks might give you ample opportunity to ask a relevant follow-up question. For example, if an interviewer seems focused on how long you intend to stay with the company and in what capacity, you might want to ask about retention and standards for promotion: the interviewer might be signaling, on the one hand, that employee turnover rates are quite high (a red flag) or promotional opportunities are there for the taking (a positive incentive).

•   Be sure to use your listening skills to perceive information that may be somewhat implicit rather than explicit. If an interviewer consistently asks about your ability to handle stressful situations, then you might rightly deduce that this is a high-pressure workplace. If an interviewer seems interested in your future professional development plans, this might signal that you are a candidate for a higher-level position. In any case, the interviewer will consciously or incidentally reveal a lot about the company. Listening to what is said will give you ample opportunity and ammunition to ask pertinent questions and make smart decisions.

• There are specific ways in which you can hone your listening skills. Let's face facts: many of us, particularly when faced with being put on the spot in a stressful situation such as a job interview, will tune out what is going on around us. Diligent observation and listening skills take some practice.

o Practice listening with a friend or family member. Ask them to tell you an unfamiliar story, then try to relay the details back to them a few hours later. Or, simply let your support group know that, in preparation for the interview, you'd like to be made aware of when you are accidentally zoning out. As long as you leave personal feelings aside, you'll likely learn a lot about how carefully you listen—or not.

o Prepare for the interview thoroughly, both in terms of practical preparation and in terms of psychological preparation. Have everything ready to go the night before (outfit, materials, travel plans), as well as conduct stress-relieving activities the day before and get a good night's sleep. The more prepared you are, the better able you are to relax enough to be a good listener.

o   Keep your materials as organized and simple as possible, so you can avoid accidental distractions. It's likely you'll miss something important if you're rooting around in your bag for a pen, for example. And remember to turn off your cell phone. One quick buzz or ring can ruin an entire interview, much less your ability to focus and listen.

o   Your body language will indicate to the interviewer how well you are listening. Show engagement by leaning toward the interviewer when he or she is speaking; nod when appropriate other such items avoid interruption. All of these silent signals reveal that you are a good listener—a boon to you during the interview process itself, and a boon to any employer who wishes to hire an employee with excellent communication skills.

o   Repeat back to the interviewer what he or she is saying in order to be certain that you have the most important details clear. This is a method by which you clearly indicate that you have been respectfully listening.

o   Don't worry if you have to ask the interviewer to repeat a question or explain something more thoroughly. Nobody is a perfect listener and that kind of diligence can prevent misunderstanding.

Steps for Follow Up

While it may appear that the process of applying for and securing your dream job is complete when the interview is over, there is still one more important step up: you should follow up appropriately. When you follow up in appropriate ways, it can have the added benefit of reminding the potential employer of why you are a strong candidate in the first place; it shows respect and attention to detail, as well as allowing you to pursue answers of your own. Here are some details about how to conduct a proper follow-up protocol.

- When should you follow up? There are two distinct answers to this: the first is that you should follow up immediately with some kind of thank you note (more on that below); the second is that you should allow an appropriate amount of time to pass before nudging the interviewer to give you some specific results. At the end of the interview itself, find an opportunity to ask when you might hear back from the company if you haven't already been told. If you don't hear back from them in the allotted time period, wait two or three more days before you send a polite email or place a polite phone call. If you aren't sure when you'll hear back, wait at least a week before checking back in. As with listening skills, a polite and professional follow up note can remind a potential employer of your qualifications, abilities, and attributes.

- How should you follow up? This, of course, will depend upon the nature of the interview and job position. It is rare, however, that you should ever follow up in person. The most common ways to follow up are with an email or a phone call, and which you choose depends on your level of confidence in speaking extemporaneously or needing to script a response. A follow-up email gives you the opportunity to compose your (concise!) thoughts before sending, though it doesn't always provide the kind of immediate gratification that you may want or need. If you decide to call the interviewer or hiring manager, be sure to jot down what you'd like to say beforehand. In either case, be sure that your tone is friendly and that you keep your remarks concise. You can also ask if they require any further materials from you in your follow up—this might be especially relevant if you are concerned that the interview did not go as well as you would have hoped or if you remembered some important information that you weren't able to convey at the time of the original interview.

• Regardless of whether you eventually need to follow up further, you should always write a quick note of thanks after the interview. While some might suggest that this is rather old-fashioned, it is still very much the case that this practice is routinely followed and clearly appreciated. The more thoughtful the note, the more successful the results. Here are some things to consider when writing that crucial thank you note:

o Be sure to write and send a thank-you note within 24 hours of the interview—any longer and it becomes a moot point. Today, most thank you notes are sent via email, but one sent via mail can garner special attention; just be sure that it is sent promptly so that you aren't forgotten in the interim. Typically, an email is a better choice because of the short time-lapse, but if you are physically close enough to stop by with a handwritten note, then that might be the best choice.

o   Address the thank you to everyone who played a role in your application process, from all the interviewers to the recruiter, when applicable. In some cases, it may be applicable to send a quick note to another employee who participated in some form, as well. In many cases, you will be directing your thank you to one specific interviewer. In other cases, if you are interviewed by a few people, then you might want to send a quick note to all involved, especially if their capacities or responsibilities in the interview differed. If you are interviewed by a full panel of people, then you might consider writing one overarching note to the person in charge, and Cc-ing everyone else.

o   A thank you note should contain a friendly and respectful greeting, using the person's name and honorific (Dr., Ms., Director, etc.), with a short paragraph expressing your appreciation for their time and effort, closing with a professional "sincerely" and your name. If you can think of specific detail from the interview that was especially striking, then you might briefly mention it in your paragraph in order to remind them of you. You also might throw in a compliment if it is sincere.

o   Essentially, your tone should be professional yet personable. Avoid emojis of any kind, and don't pepper the note with exclamation points or overly excitable adjectives and adverbs. There are numerous templates available online should you wish to review some.

• Finally, know when to move on: if you have sent a thank you note and have made two attempts at follow up without response, then it is time to start preparing for your next interview. Be patient, however, and space out your follow up over the course of a couple of weeks: thank you note immediately, follow up within a few days of when a response was anticipated, and one final follow up a week or so after that. If there is no response within a month, then your time and energy are best spent moving on.

Chapter 8: Sample Q&A: Some Tough Questions and Ready Answers

Throughout this guide, we have reviewed the various types of interview questions, techniques for answering, and looked at various examples of questions and answers. In this final chapter, we will look at what most experts consider to be the toughest interview questions—either because they steer a candidate into negative territory or they run the risk of producing a rambling, pointless answer. We will also take a quick look at some interview questions that cross the line: you should be aware of what you are allowed not to answer during an interview, legally and ethically speaking.

Remember, interviewers like to ask tough questions—indeed, it is their job to do so—in order to give you the opportunity to reveal the best parts of yourself. Don't think of these tough questions as deliberate attempts to trip you up, as obstacles; rather, think of them as clear examples of your opportunity to show how professional and poised you are, how logical and/or creative your thought process is, and how you handle pressure in the moment. Take the view that the interview is, truly and ultimately, in your control: with proper preparation, you should be ready to tackle even the toughest questions with clear and ready answers.

• Common to most interviews, the question about weakness will inevitably be asked, in some form or another. "What critical feedback do you receive most often?" is just another version of the same kind of question. This kind of question poses a pitfall because it asks you to reveal something negative about yourself, which certainly leaves us feeling vulnerable, especially in an interview situation. It also poses a pitfall in that you might either avoid the question or forget to steer into positive territory. In the first instance, a candidate might respond by suggesting that the critical feedback he's ever received has been inconsequential; this comes across as arrogant and/or lacking in self-awareness. In the second instance, you reveal a flaw without indicating that you are working on it. The best answer acknowledges that you have a weakness—this indicates self-awareness and humility—and reveals specific and concrete actions that you have been taking to improve—focusing and ending on the positive.

• In a similar vein, potential employers will also often ask about an obstacle that you have overcome in the past. This, again, invites the uncomfortable proposition that you reveal something difficult and/or negative from your past. Nevertheless, if you are prepared with a STAR ready answer, providing details about the situation, tasks, actions, and results that shows how you ultimately overcame said obstacle, then you are actually telling an inspiring story about both your professional abilities and your personal attributes. Telling a story that combines the use of your hard skills and soft skills is the strongest way to approach this kind of question.

• Because stress is a component of every professional experience, employers will often want to test your facility for handling it, so you should expect a question about how you deal with stress or pressure. Again, don't make the mistake of suggesting that you never get stressed out or that you deal with stress just fine. This is clearly skirting the truth, and the employer knows it. Rather, construct a specific example wherein you acknowledge that you felt enormous pressure (of deadline, on your skillset, or other) but took steps to deal with that stress to overcome it. Make sure that you reveal the results (STAR method, again) of your process: showing that even though you almost buckled under stress but ended up figuring out a way to deal with it and overcome it—to positive ends—is a satisfying and inspiring story.

• Another potential pitfalls are questions that ask you to comment about your personal experience with management or colleagues. An interviewer might ask what your worst experience was or to describe a conflict that happened in your previous experience. Certainly, you should approach the question with honesty—but also with a healthy dose of tact. An employer wants to know what kind of person and/or management style you work best with, of course, but he or she doesn't really want to know that about past squabbles or the personal foibles of others. Avoid any personal references, names, or other information that might tip the interviewer off to a particular person about whom you might be discussing.

Indeed, it is best not to discuss others when answering the question, in general. Instead, come up with a specific example wherein a negative experience—a clash of personalities, or a conflict of interests—created a temporarily difficult working situation, emphasis on the temporary. You want to end the story with how it was resolved in as positive a manner as possible.

• If you are currently employed by another company within the industry, then you will most likely be asked about why you are leaving your current job. This question proffers a possible landmine of inappropriate responses, just as with the above question. This is not the time to get personal or to use the interview as a chance to complain about another company, boss, or colleague. Instead, it is the opportunity for you to offer your potential employer an honest assessment of what wasn't working for you in your current position that encouraged you to seek a job elsewhere. Tactful honesty is the best policy here, as well. Try to frame your response in the most positive terms available: "I have thoroughly enjoyed my work with X Company, but at this time, professional growth opportunities are few. I wanted to begin thinking about career advancement at this moment in my professional life, so this job offered me the chance to best use my many skills."

• You will also often be asked a question about either why you wish to work for this employer or why this employer should feel compelled to hire you. These are similar questions, and they are tough questions because you don't know who your competition is or what, exactly, management is looking for. In the first instance, the best preparation you can do for your answer is to conduct adequate research into the company overall; the more you know about what the company does and how its culture functions, the better able you are to make a pitch about your enthusiasm and fittingness for the job. In the second instance, you are essentially being asked how your particular skill set matches the position; review the original job description and apply your knowledge gained from researching the company as a whole. Review your list of skills and make a clear link between each skill and a component of the job qualifications or expectations. You might also prepare a specific example, with concrete details, about how a particular experience makes you uniquely suited for the job—this is a way of setting yourself apart from the other candidates.

• Another difficult question you might get is to talk about your greatest regrets and/or your greatest achievements: as with questions about weaknesses and strengths, be sure you have a ready answer prepared that doesn't swing too hard to the negative or dwell too much on the arrogance. Showing an ability to learn from regrets is the best approach in that scenario, while relaying one specific achievement in the context of your professional life is the best way to show success without arrogance. Stick to one example that is specific to one past experience.

- Finally, beware of some questions that skirt the line between what is allowable in an interview scenario:

  o An employer is allowed to ask your address but not whether you rent or own, nor are they allowed to ask with whom you live.

  o An employer is allowed to ask about age only in the context of requirements for the job (such as working as a bartender). Otherwise, they are not allowed to ask what year you were born or when you graduated high school.

  o Beware of probing questions regarding availability, as well: while not always illegal, these kinds of questions can be used to screen for religious affiliation (can you work weekends?) or to discriminate against parents (do you have evening childcare?).

  o Citizenship questions can be asked in certain scenarios, but only in the context of "are you legally permitted to work in the United States?" An employer cannot ask citizenship status, legally speaking.

  o Questions about credit and finances are also not permitted, such as "do you have a bank or savings account?"

  o If asked about a disability, only answer if it is relevant to the position to which you are applying.

  o Basically, know your rights before you enter the interview space to best protect your privacy and candidacy.

- In general, all interview questions can feel like tough questions, and the best way in which you can handle them is through preparation and practice. Answering questions with specific examples, using concrete details, rather than employing vague generalities will enable you to tackle any tough question with aplomb. Your dream job is just a few questions and answers away!

Chapter 9: Credential Verification and Qualifications

Among the simplest kinds of questions you may be asked at a job interview, credential verification questions ask you to verify the details provided on your resume and/or within your cover letter. If you are a recent graduate, these kinds of questions might ask you to discuss your course work, intern opportunities, and extracurricular endeavors, as well as specific grade point averages or other measurable markers of accomplishment. If you have work experience, the questions might focus instead on your tenure at a particular company or your specific positions held, promotions gained, and projects completed. Whatever direction these questions take, they require you to be prepared and well-versed in the details of your educational experience and/or work history. Essentially, you are being asked to vouch for your qualifications objectively and honestly.

Credential verification questions can do a couple of things in the course of an interview: first, they can allow for a breaking of the ice at the beginning, in order to allow both interviewer and candidate to warm up to the process; second, they can serve as a jumping-off point to elaborate on particular achievements in your educational or work history that will illustrate your fittingness for the job; third, they can give you the opportunity to explain away any gaps or unconventional issues with your resume.

First, credential questions can be a way to ease into the interview, allowing for everybody to settle in and relax a bit. Because these kinds of questions essentially ask you to review and verify your resume, be sure that you have a copy quick at hand in case you need to quickly look at something. Otherwise, you should be able to readily answer these kinds of questions without hesitation. The interviewer may ask a series of verification questions or just one or two that he or she is interested in; partly, this depends on how detailed your resume is in the first place. If certain credentials are of greater interest to your potential employer, then this serves as a way into broader issues, as follows.

Second, certain credentials might encourage interviewers to ask some follow up questions: for example, they might be interested in knowing why you stayed for so long (or so short) at a particular place of employment; or, they might be interested in knowing how certain kinds of coursework were relevant to your overall educational achievement. They might also use credential questions to prompt you to show a link between various activities and interests you've engaged with in the past: that is, you might be encouraged to show how seemingly disparate parts of your overall credential portfolio actually link together. Say you've been working as a graphic designer and you also list that you volunteered at a food pantry: these credentials don't necessarily seem to have anything to do with one another. You should be prepared to show how you have learned skills from each that complement the other. Additionally, credential verification questions could lead to the interviewer following up on how these past credentials might serve the current position for which you are applying. That is, you might be asked not only how your credentials have reinforced your growing skillset through past experience but also how these credentials link to the requirements being asked of you for the current job.

Third, when an interviewer asks credential verification questions, he or she might be giving you the opportunity to explain or justify particular gaps in your resume. For example, if there is a gap in employment, then the interviewer might ask you what you were doing during that time and why the gap exists in the first place. In this case, be very prepared to answer honestly and thoroughly. For another example, the gap in your resume might be related to a particular set of skills. An interviewer can use a credential verification question to prompt you to expand on the kind of soft skills—leadership, effective communication, conflict resolution—needed to fulfill the requirements of a particular position. It can also be a prompt for you to expand upon a specific promotion or project. Finally, when reviewing your resume, an interviewer might candidly ask why certain skills seem to be missing. Be prepared to explain this, as well, and demonstrate how you intend to develop this skill or fill in your resume's gaps.

Beyond those opportunities, credential verification questions are also closely related to qualification questions. In this case, you are being asked to expand upon how your credentials and experience make you qualified for the position at hand. Your credentials reveal your qualifications in a concise and concrete way; however, the qualifications you possess represent more than mere credentials but also general work and life experience, in addition to the possession of a variety of soft skills that will assist you with any position you might want to tackle.

For example, if it isn't abundantly clear from your resume and cover letter why are qualified for the position, then you need to be prepared to show how your experience—while seemingly tangential—does actually apply. This is relevant when you are just starting out your career or when you are trying to make a shift in careers. This is also one of the reasons why relaying your soft skills is so important: soft skills carry over to whatever job you might be wanting, from adaptability and flexibility to dependability and attitude. For example, if you have worked in a non-profit environment and you are switching to a corporate position, then you need to be able to elaborate on how the skills at a non-profit might translate. This could be as concrete as suggesting that developing strong accounting skills is necessary at a non-profit, where budgets can be tight, will assist you in helping generate more profitability in a corporate setting. Or, it could be as abstract as revealing that your communication skills in your work at the non-profit will easily transfer to the corporate world; writing a newsletter to potential donors requires the same skill set as composing coherent and concise interdepartmental memos.

On the other hand, you might be asked to explain why you are applying for a job that you appear to be overqualified for: say you have a master's degree, yet you are applying for an entry-level position. Many factors would determine your answer, but do prepared to explain. It might be that you are shifting careers or industries, as in the example above, or it might be that you are interested in a greater balance between life and work, so you are scaling back your responsibilities. It might be that you are simply passionate about the opportunity afforded by this particular position and are willing to accept a lower-level position in order to get a foot in the door. These kinds of questions might also apply if you have been in management-level positions but are currently seeking a non-managerial job.

Qualification questions might also ask you to go into detail about certain abilities that you list or infer on your resume or cover letter. Why is it that you feel you have a particular facility for XXX? Or, what do you think are your greatest strengths (concomitantly, weaknesses)? This might also take the form of asking you why you are the best candidate for the position: that is, what is about your credentials and your broader qualifications makes you better than any other candidate who will interview? Be sure to prepare some sort of answer for this question beforehand, choosing something from your past educational, work, or life experience that is truly unique to you—or, be able to show how, in the aggregate, the skills and experiences you have are greater than the sum of their parts. Some specific ideas of how to deal with qualification questions will be addressed later in this guide.

These are just a few of the kind of qualification questions you might be asked to relay during an interview: others might address what you consider to be challenging (again, this speaks to potential gaps in credentials or skills) or press you to justify how your experience and qualifications will impact the company's productivity and bottom line. Many qualification questions veer into experience verification questions, which are discussed in the following chapter.

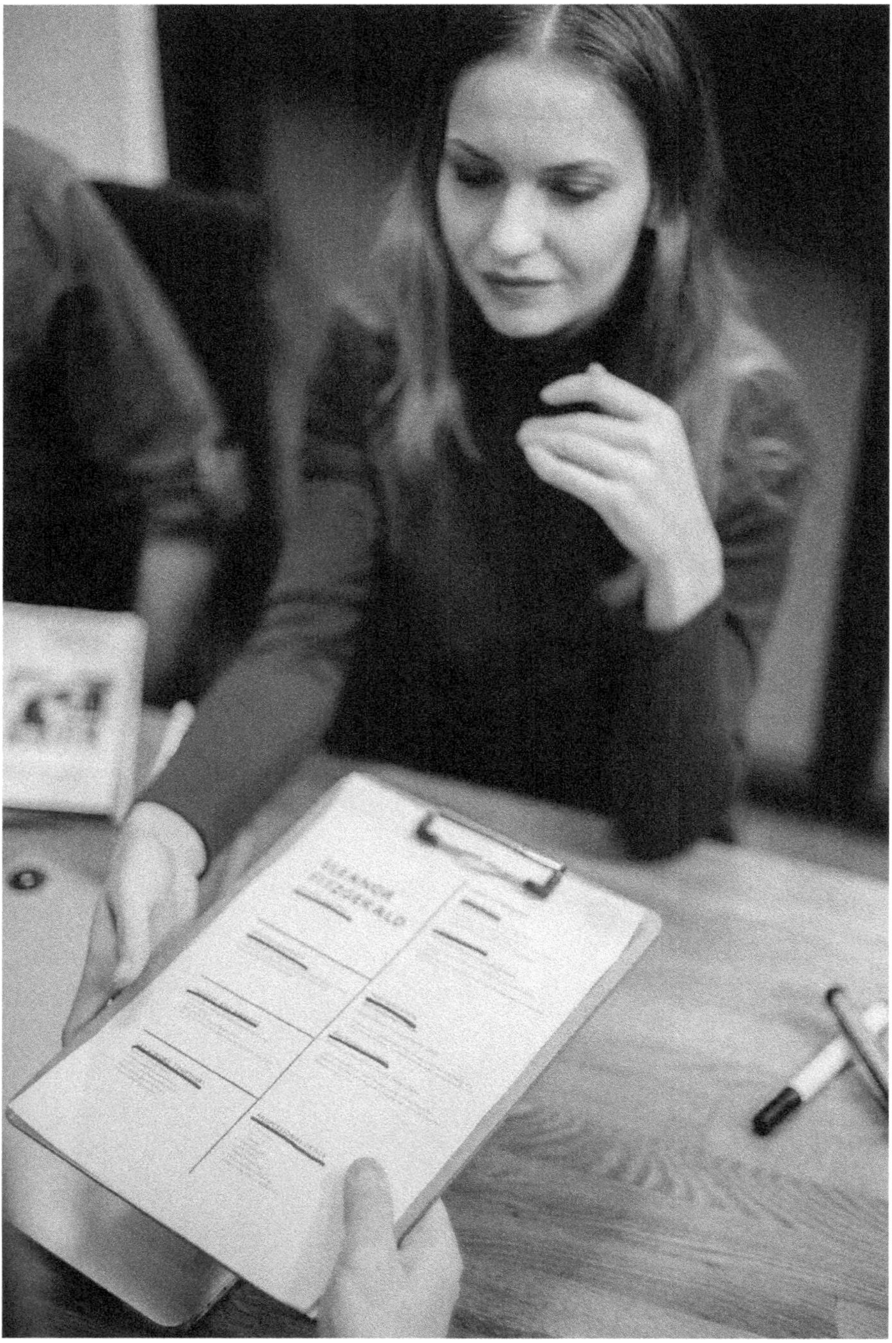

Chapter 10: Communication Skills

Obviously, possessing effective communication skills is crucial to any interview or professional position: you must have basic writing abilities, effective oral communication strategies, as well as acceptable interpersonal skills. In addition, listening skills are an oft-forgotten, yet equally crucial, component in effective communication. These skills are in display from the beginning of any job search: your resume and cover letter will reveal how well you communicate in writing, while the job interview itself will showcase how effectively you communicate orally, as well as how attuned you are to good listening. See below for a refresher review of the basic components of effective communication skills.

Writing Abilities

• Obviously, the first piece of information that you must create before you even attempt getting the job interview is the resume. After you have acquired the skills, education, and experience necessary to secure your ideal job, you have to be able to put them into a professional, easily readable, and impressive compilation that is called the resume. Think about how each and every one of your experiences can apply to something in the job that you are applying to—and, yes, you should customize your resume for each job for which you apply. If you don't necessarily have a lot of working experience—say, you are a recent college graduate—then you need to show how other activities you have done (volunteering, interning, hobbies) will translate well into the professional arena.

- To get started, seek out sample resumes from across the internet or from other job platforms. You need not worry about building a great resume from scratch; there are any number of templates available at many different sites that can get you started. Be sure to match the template with your field, as you don't want an academic curriculum vitae if you are applying for a standard job in business, and vice versa (just for one example).

- Once you find a template that you think is right for your particular set of skills and your field, then be sure to spend adequate time customizing it. You don't want such a generic resume that you won't stand out in the field of other candidates. Also think about your own personal style and how you can show that—within reason and with professionalism—on your particular resume.

- Also consider how you organize your resume, for there are many different ways in which you can relay the material. Most often, resumes are organized chronological, listing educational and professional achievements and positions in the order at which they occurred, from most recent on down. But you could also create a different type of resume, if you have a different set of skills and experience: a functional resume, for instance, lists skills and abilities with relevant examples, instead of listing them in chronological order (this might be a good idea if your work experience is limited); a targeted resume will have you specifically "target" your abilities and past experience to the exact job that you want, following closely on the original request for employment. And, of course, a combination resume puts these different methods together. Think about what is the best fit for you and for this particular job.

• The resume itself should be simple and easy to read: most hiring managers will merely skim a resume, rather than read it thoroughly, so the more able you are to make the most important information the most prominent, that better serves your purpose. Some basic formatting tips and techniques are as follows:

o use a basic font, as discussed above;

o don't justify your margins, which creates odd gaps in formatting;

o keep dates and other numbers aligned to the right;

o use digits when employing numbers (10, rather than ten);

o avoid centering any information;

o use boldface to highlight either the company for whom you worked or your respective roles at previous workplaces, but not both;

o avoid all caps;

o when using bullet points, keep it to two lines or less;

o   employ a separate section for skills, so prospective employers can read through quickly;

o   and be consistent in formatting throughout your resume, leaving some white space for ease of reading.

•   There is no need to include a list of references on your resume itself; if you get the job interview, the interviewer will expect that you have references, and you should be prepared to provide them.

•   Next, your writing abilities will be showcased in your cover letter, of course. Not all jobs require a cover letter, but most skilled professional jobs do. Even if you're not asked to provide a cover letter, a brief and well-written expression of interest in and qualification for the job would not be misplaced.

•   While this may not be the advice that many applicants wish to hear, it is the best possible advice: you should craft an individual and specific cover letter for each position to which you apply. In a typical three paragraph letter, this would mean changing details in the first paragraph regarding the position itself, and writing your second paragraph—the bulk of the cover letter—about your skills, qualifications, experiences, and enthusiasm for this particular job. Address the cover letter personally and professionally to your interviewer, hiring manager, or potential employer, when possible. You should also do some research into the company itself, so that you have some idea of the bigger picture; this is addressed later in this book.

- There are always templates available online, as with resumes, so don't hesitate to use one of these, or at least review some of them to get a better idea of how to begin and develop your cover letter. When opening the letter, try to move beyond the intentionally generic "I am writing to apply for X position with X company"—this is dull and reveals a potential lack of enthusiasm on your part.

- While "To Whom It May Concern" is still a standard in the annals of writing to someone you don't personally know, when addressing a cover letter, strive to make it somewhat more specific, such as "Dear Hiring Manager" or "To the Department of X at Company X." This simply shows that you aren't recycling a rehashed letter for multiple jobs.

- Use the cover letter to review more of your work history and experience than what is revealed in your resume; that is, be careful to simply repeat what is already listed on your resume. Start thinking, instead, about particular activities in which you participated in a professional capacity that reveal something special about you as an employee. Illustrate what skills this task asked you to utilize, talk about what was accomplished as a result, and think about what soft skills you were also called upon to use. Getting down to this specific level will not only make you a stronger candidate, but will also serve to help you begin to prepare for the interview itself.

- Avoid the pitfall of talking about how much this job would mean to you—sure, that's in your self-interest, but your potential employer doesn't necessarily care. Instead, focus on what you would bring to the job and to the larger company as a whole. The intention is to show how well you would fit into a particular position at this specific company.

• This is also the place where you can make a case for the fact that you would be an ideal fit for the position—even if your work history doesn't necessarily reveal that. This is especially important in a cover letter that you write for a job that takes you off your beaten career path, or if you are writing a cover letter for your first big job out of graduation. You need to be able to show how your training and skills and personality are equal to the task of whatever this job might have on hand. That said, link any experience directly to the job, when at all possible.

• You also want to strike a balance in your tone. Of course, a cover letter should be succinct and professional, but it shouldn't be overly stiff or formal. You want some part of your personality to show, as well. When you are excessively formal, you appear stiff and distant, while too much conversational personality can appear flippant and inappropriate. You want to both approachable while maintaining a professional demeanor.

• You should also employ the research you have done on the company in the cover letter itself, using key words and other lingo that will reflect your knowledge of the company at large. Peruse the web site and social media for the company and employ some of the key words and/or phrases used there; don't overdo, of course, or you risk sounding too sycophantic.

• Finally, you must EDIT your cover letter carefully and thoroughly; have an English savvy friend or colleague help you out if necessary. Cover letters with grammatical or syntactical difficulties undermine any good they can possibly do. One bit of advice for any writing you may do in your professional career: READ IT ALOUD before you conduct a final edit and turn it in. Reading aloud can help you capture the tone (is it too stiff and formal? Too conversational?) and flow (is it too rambling? well organized?), as well as alert you to mistakes (if you're gasping for breath at the end of a sentence, then it probably needs some editing). When you enter the interview space, you should know your cover letter as well as you know yourself—indeed, because that is what it is, a reflection of yourself—and be prepared to elaborate on in material within it.

• For more detailed guidelines to the resume and cover letter part of the job interview process, see my book Job Interview Preparation.

Effective Oral Communication

• Clearly, the interview itself is designed for you to showcase your oral communication skills. One of the best ways that you can ensure that you are revealing your skills in the most effective manner possible is to prepare and practice for the interview, following the tips and techniques as outlined in Chapter 4. You can also find more in-depth guidelines to how to prepare for interview questions and answers in my book, Interview Q&A.

• Another way in which you can demonstrate effective oral communication is in how you manage yourself: body language and other non-verbal cues fill in the blanks in any interview (or, really, any) situation. See the guidelines for how to conduct yourself professionally to understand how to telegraph the correct cues during an interview.

• You will also want to learn how to manage your stress levels. A lot of people's greatest fear is that they will say the wrong thing. To avoid this pitfall, remind yourself that this is actually quite a simple stressor to overcome. Keep it simple: avoid profanity or offensive language and just be yourself. That's really all the advice you need to conquer that particular fear.

• While in the interview, if you need a moment to compose yourself, then take it. Ask the interviewer to repeat a question, or rephrase the question back to him or her to give you a chance to think about it before answering; take a sip of water; check in with the interviewer that you've fully answered a given question. There's nothing wrong with allowing yourself a moment of time to think. It's perfectly acceptable to say, "That is a really good question. Let me think about that for a moment."

• Also remember that almost all questions offer you the opportunity to reveal something positive about yourself, in addition to the obstacle of inadvertently showcasing something negative about yourself. If you are asked about your strengths, then you should obviously address particular skills, either hard or soft, that you have demonstrated in specific and concrete ways in the past. It is not enough to say that you have "very effective communication skills"; you need to be able to reveal how you have specifically used those skills in past positions: "I think that one of my greatest strengths is my effective communication skills, which I demonstrated in writing the annual report and providing press releases to the media." Or, "My effective communication skills led to a role within the team as mediator in solving problems and conflicts." With regard to a hard skill, you might show how your facility with programming led to a specific promotion or a coveted position on a high level team; in this case, describe the specific project and your role in it. Still, displaying one's strengths takes some humility and finesse: if you come across as a braggart—"I was the best salesperson the company had ever seen"—then you are effectively undermining your candidacy.

Interpersonal Skills

• Professionally speaking, interpersonal skills reveal how an employee engages and interacts with those around her, and they are a sign of emotional intelligence and the ability to communicate effectively. While not always directly related to written, oral, or aural skills, the ways in which these interpersonal skills are relayed is through these communication outlets. Interpersonal skills show how an employee is motivated and how he or she uses knowledge and analysis to get the best results in a given professional situation.

• Specifically, interpersonal skills consist of several elements: displaying self-confidence; maintaining a strong work ethic; fostering the ability to work well with others; sustaining dependability; demonstrating openness to others and to feedback; collaborating well with others; and showing appreciation and positivity.

• Again, a great deal of interpersonal skills is covered by maintaining a professional etiquette as discussed in Chapter 5.

The Importance of Listening

• It is potentially the case that listening is one of the most underestimated skills that is necessary for a job interview. Showcasing solid listening skills will make you appear empathetic, engaged, intelligent, and enthusiastic. While you should certainly practice your answers to potential questions as detailed earlier in this guide, you should avoid spouting off practiced answers without truly listening to what the interviewer is requesting. An interview should have an ebb and flow like a conversation, and while much of it will be focused on you, be sure to allow yourself time and space to listen and absorb what is going on at the other side of the equation.

• Be sure to use your listening skills to perceive information that may be somewhat implicit rather than explicit. If an interviewer consistently asks about your ability to handle stressful situations, then you might rightly deduce that this is a high pressure workplace. If an interviewer seems interested in your future professional development plans, this might signal that you are a candidate for a higher level position. In any case, the interviewer will consciously or incidentally reveal a lot about the company. Listening to what is said will give you ample opportunity and ammunition to ask pertinent questions and make smart decisions.

• There are specific ways in which you can hone your listening skills. Let's face facts: many of us, particularly when faced with being put on the spot in a stressful situation such as a job interview, will tune out what is going on around us. Diligent observation and listening skills take some practice.

o Practice listening with a friend or family member. Ask them to tell you an unfamiliar story, then try to relay the details back to them a few hours later. Or, simply let your support group know that, in preparation for the interview, you'd like to be made aware of when you are accidentally zoning out. As long as you leave personal feelings aside, you'll likely learn a lot about how carefully you listen—or not.

o Prepare for the interview thoroughly, both in terms of practical preparation and in terms of psychological preparation. Have everything ready to go the night before (outfit, materials, travel plans), as well as conduct stress relieving activities the day before and get a good night's sleep. The more prepared you are, the better able you are to relax enough to be a good listener.

o   Keep your materials as organized and simple as possible, so you can avoid accidental distractions. It's likely you'll miss something important if you're rooting around in your bag for a pen, for example. And remember to turn off your cell phone. One quick buzz or ring can ruin an entire interview, much less your ability to focus and listen.

o   Your body language will indicate to the interviewer how well you are listening. Show engagement by leaning toward the interviewer when he or she is speaking; nod when appropriate; and avoid interruption. All of these silent signals reveal that you are a good listener—a boon to you during the interview process itself, and a boon to any employer who wishes to hire an employee with excellent communication skills.

o   Repeat back to the interviewer what he or she is saying in order to be certain that you have the most important details clear. This is a method by which you clearly indicate that you have been respectfully listening.

Conclusion

A job interview is potentially a life-altering event. You have been searching for your ideal job, amassing skills and experience along the way to help you secure what you need for professional success and personal satisfaction. While an excellent resume and cover letter will enable you to secure a foot in the door, the interview itself also requires a particular set of skills and some significant amount of practice for it to be as successful as possible. Employers often consider the interview a litmus test not only for how an employee will be productive and valuable at specific work-related tasks but also for how an employee will fit in with the corporate culture and be a productive team member beyond the technical skills they bring. As such, you should treat the job interview as a process much like an educational or training opportunity. It requires research and knowledge, experiential training, and practice to be good at job interviews. This guide has provided you with a plethora of tools you can utilize in order to become the most attractive candidate out of many. Not only have you honed your resume and cover letter writing skills, but you have also learned how to research a company, outline your story, and reduce the stress associated with the intense process of securing your dream job. From looking and acting professionally to being thoroughly prepared for any style of interview, any kind of question, you know now how to demonstrate that you have both the hard and soft skills that will make you a valuable employee to any industry or company.

Ultimately, the importance of a job interview really cannot be overstated: this simple act is the culmination of your years of hard work, focus, and energy. You may have paid tens of thousands of dollars for a higher education or special training just to get to this point; you may have spent your entire life dreaming of this particular job in this particular field; you may have an inkling that this job might be able to propel you to success and security in ways you have heretofore only dreamed of. The job interview is one way in which to gain entry into whatever elite group of which you've always wanted to be a part.

CPSIA information can be obtained
at www.ICGtesting.com
Printed in the USA
BVHW041206010321
601386BV00008B/642